A few
Contemporary
Inspirations
from some of the
'Selected Sayings'
(Analects)
Of Confucius

*

(based on translations
by Arthur Waley)

*

Traumear

"He who by reanimating the old
can gain knowledge of the new
is fit to be a teacher."
(Book II, 11)

*

*

These are inspirations based on those Analects, or 'sayings' of Confucius of which they bear the number. I have used the translations by Arthur Waley.

I have chosen only a few of those Analects that interested me from Books I to IV. There are XX books altogether, but sadly I soon ran out of inspiration – which does not imply that the rest are not worth reading.

These pieces, as I present them here, are not translations or transcriptions but more or less what I would call transubstantiations. I do not mean: This is what the ancient Chinese sage or his disciples really said or meant but rather: This is how he might express his thought if he lived in the post modern or contemporary world, with access to what has become available in our time, not in terms of culture and civilization but of true knowledge, understanding and ethical spirit as I see it. Also, it makes little difference to me whether these sayings really stem from Confucius in person. What matters to me is the availability of substance.

From Book 1

1

That none recognize your merit,
Let this be the strengthener.
What if all your days were for such in-
crease?
When the cup runs over
Does the cup seek credit for it?
Such are the pursuits of the old,
The rewards of him who waits.

Then there is he who follows,
Who seeks out what is new.
Renounced energy, harnessed energy.
At the fork of the road
Do not hesitate but choose.
An unsung hymn to the earth –
The eloquence of the silent places.

*

2

Truly commendable : the wish to do good.
Not at the end of the rope
But where it is tied, fixed,
There the knot is carefully fashioned.
Authority that is not delegated
But rooted in the soil due to suffering
May take issue with the authorities
But never unkindly, impolitely.

Impotence of speech, impotence of behaviour –
One is more frightful than the other,
And yet precisely in such straits
You may drink from the well of goodness.
While crippled, learn new skills of movement;
During the race placidly recline.
Even conduct towards relatives and relations
Is embraced by service of the good.

*

3

Let your talk be compassionate
And your speech to the point.
Let your aim be communication
Not justification of self.
Foolish talk is disease
And rambling speech a pitfall.

Let your manner be unassuming
And your conduct kindly.
Let your aim be peace
Not advertisement of self.
A pretentious manner breeds malice
And indifferent conduct discontent.

*

4

Our true interest lies
    In consideration for others;
A word spoken to a friend
    Is worth a hundred to a crowd.

    But I ask myself this?
    The enemy rising against me,
    Am I not to consider him
    Worthy of my word?
    Or the friend who mistakes his interests
    And bargains for my soul,
    Am I not to hate him?

On examining my conduct
    I learn from the experience;
Examining my self
    I miserably lose myself.

*

5

What today counts as energy
Is a psychic phenomenon;
In the lazy man it sickens,
In the ostentatious man it destroys.

Energy invested early in the morning
Makes for a day of cheerful activity;
Not a minute is wasted,
No task is unseasonal.
Both persons and thing are allotted
Their appropriate expenditure of care.

Those who psyche themselves up,
Though they suppose they do good,
Raise havoc and cause harm
By disturbing the natural balance.
Thirst is not quenched by foam,
The flapping of wings is not flight.

While my nature sees to its affairs,
Who am I to demand or to impose?
A man takes care of himself
By both doing and being.

*

6

A young man's duty (this never changes)
Is to form an attitude of respect towards his elders,
Regardless of how they behave towards him,
For respect not only opens the way for him
But equally protects him against insult and ridicule.

A kindly disposition towards all is difficult
But well worth cultivating. The sooner he learns
To overcome his annoyance, his rage, the better.
It will keep his soul free of acrimony, of resent-
ment.

Then let him seek the intimacy of the good.
No better way to succeed here than by
Relinquishing the rights and justifications of self,
Since these bar the ever-present influence of the
good.
Then he may remain wide awake for surprises.

Though these comprise the chief virtues of a youth,
None of them are touched on by State Education.
The modern ambition is to divert all attention
Away from duty and alas! towards vanity.

*

The educated man –
He knows from within how to cope
And he has not learned but he learns.
Show me such a one.
Here we have a unique human being.
You cannot predict his reaction,
(No buttons to push).
He will have his priorities,
His primary and secondary motives.
Looking back on himself, he smiles.
Looking around, he perceives calmly,
Looking ahead, he becomes alert.
Will he frown upon his mortality?
No more than he will scoff at his eternal life.
Can anything not substantial
Have a face and an obverse side?
Turning to his betters he defers,
Those who also seek the good he reveres;
Adultery he abhors.

*

When first we seek the truth within
And are drawn by it,
So that its spirit demands our addiction
And we may choose to put all our eggs
    in that one basket,
Then we do well to shun all those who are
    indifferent to the truth.
However do not make a thing of it,
For it happens in any case,
Since the truth itself is exclusive,
Remaining unfamiliar to those who shun it.

In search of the truth remain
Serious but flexible.
Linger not over apparent mistakes
But press on, ever mindful
Of the next move to be made.
Who will be your guide?
What little truth you discover.
Act on it, work it out,
At first solely for the purpose of
A sound inward foundation.
Later you may build in reality.

*

9

Once we have joined the living
What are the dead to us?
Behold, the dead disappear from the
    surface of the earth
While the living are with us always.
Much has changed.
Where once there was a people, or a tribe,
Now the apple is peeled, cored and sliced.
Where once the idea called Man held sway,
Now practicality demands we speak
    of men, women and children.
These are not dead and they do not die,
    let us be adamant,
But they turn a corner and reappear
    where we cannot point to them,
Nor would we wish to, since they have chosen
In life that communal eternality of hearts.
Within the morality of love
We pick no quarrel with the dead
But our life flows over them,
If they should wake and perceive.

*

10

Assume that every stranger
Is a repository of new life.
Mass media, a common market,
Make people more alike,
So our task is to cultivate the differences.

During any genuine exchange
Cultural forces are unleashed
And all too readily misunderstood.
Fear cripples authenticity, so
Our task is to ease the tension.

Trust that the stranger cannot harm you.
Caution sharpens trust,
Compassion empowers it.
In a world where cowardice flourishes
Our task is to instil trust.

The sheep know the good shepherd.
Defer to the god who would
Speak from the stranger's mouth.
Our task is to practice
The courtesy of the heart.

*

11

Piety towards dead ancestors,
Then time passes, followed by
Piety towards family and tribe,
And more time passes, followed by
Piety towards the father who is spirit.

The living god is our origin.
Let us see now who can pass
From youth to maturity steadfast,
Bearing up to his mortality,
Then giving in to the death that is over-
come.

During our youth we are guided,
Often by ghosts haphazardly,
Tutored by the offspring of the blind.
A word here, a gesture there
Arouse discontent with the status quo.

Help those who know this discontent.
If a young man for three years follows
In the footsteps of him who would
Show him eternal life, then he is
Truly a son of his father.

*

12

The dramatic art of behaviour called
Ritual has as its true end harmony.
May it remain in the hands of
Those with no ulterior motives!

Those few who are now still
Generally outcast or anonymous
Have the insight into affairs,
Are capable of true government.

First the muddy waters must settle;
A new configuration of elements,
A reformation of seasons –
Minute changes usher in the cosmos.

Art as manipulation of ego and psyche
Is not true art which stems
From the recreated inward life
In the face of trial and tribulation.

Morals and manners are conduct,
Care and attention are behaviour.
Be sure that a benefit is available
When once again things go amiss.

*

13

Much depends on our origin.
However the way we behave
Is entirely up to us.
Let moods become religion,
Wildness consideration
And indifference care.
You can do what you wish,
Provided you cut no corners.
As you search for the truth
You have no time to be kind,
Neither will you be cruel.
Nevertheless those whose kindness
Is a mask for falsehood
Will charge you with cruelty.
Therefore love even your enemy.
Cleave to the truth in person
And keep his word as recorded.
Honour is a matter of
The regenerate heart.
A wife whose priority is truth
May seem to cause you pain
But remember that you both
Are to arrive at the same moment,
Each in tact as a person.

*

14

Within some of us grows
The human reality
In orderly fashion,
While we attend to our nature –
In the world around us.
We learn the way of
Perfected human nature.
A sober mind is essential,
Therefore we avoid whatever would
Cloud our awareness,
Undermine our power
Or impair our will.

Learning how to know,
Knowing how to learn
Occupies the forefront of our minds.
Faithful appetite is crucial.
Speech influences this most,
Bending it this way and that,
Strengthening resolve
Or enfeebling potency.
Faults are corrected
Not by tinkering with volition
But by overcoming their consequences.
Be guided by one who knows the way.

*

15

Instead of voiding extremes let us
Practice creation from inwardness.
However, does he who knows the way
Have much to say to the rich man,
To the one encumbered by possession;
Or for that matter to the poor man,
To the one hankering after possession?
Inward and then outward creativity
Is the province not of the possession-oriented
But of him who desires to possess the orientation
On his way from death to rebirth.

Not sufficient to adhere to the
Traditional rationale of legality
If the direction beckons, and the way.
Having cut, now file.
Having loved your kin, your friend,
Proceed now to love your enemy,
Overcoming the inward block.
Within the context of historic
Civilization and Society,
The best possible is preparation.
Now, now let us sing the ancient
Songs of future salvation.

*

16

The merit lies in what a man can do,
And what a shame it is not to be used –
Good spirit pines without utility.

A good man is a tenuous piece of myth
And no such thing exists upon the earth
But there are those who practice doing good.

A common thing to like is to be praised
But better for us if we speak the truth
And when they flinch we speak the truth
again.

A practiced eye that looks into the heart
Discovers quickly the merit of a man,
Not to admire him, but to involve him in
work.

*

from Book II

1

A powerful man
Is not afraid to do good
When it makes him unpopular,
Is not reluctant to speak the truth
When falsehood has convicted him.
Whence this power?

There is the baptism by water,
When mind and body are cleansed
By disciplined application to the truth.
There is the baptism by fire,
When our soul is cleansed
Of evil and inertia
By submission to the influence of love.

When the time is ripe
The secret is revealed.
Then the elements obey.
Then the living word is spoken
Straight into hearts
And matter is divided
As energy and dross.

Eventually the disc called world
Rotates around that single perception
And those whose influence is change
Open to good spirit.

*

2

Behold the field of creation
Patient for the work of a man!
Learn to behold and soon you will be
Certain as to your function on earth.

Add nothing, take nothing away.
With a singular look
Redeem the injustices
Against creation in the past.

When the reins are placed in your hands
You recoil, it cannot be otherwise.
Ruling, you may not neglect past experience.
Is the past not an error?

Behold, he comes on the clouds of heaven
In strength, and you will invest that strength.
His glory revives or destroys
Depending on your nonsense or substance.

How and where do you apply yourself?
Recognize the leverage you intend.
Would you cling to the effects of your motivation?
Have your feelings still power to involve you?

Do you mistake your opinions for the truth?
Do you resent your mortality?
Do you misjudge your immortality?
Behold the wonder that is you!

*

3

A human being among people
Must trust in order to get by.
There is no relying on legality,
No safety in contracts.

Human beings are exceptional,
They master by means of morality.
People are driven,
So they need to be mastered.

A man masters his popularity
But honours his humanity.
When people are trusted
The humanity in them can come alive.

Reluctantly a human being applies
Force or constraint.
People take delight in the
Unquestionable sensation of magic.

Community and conversation
Annihilate the phantoms of popularity.
Proper respect for the other one
Safeguards my own soul.

*

4

At sixty,
Though I know nothing can kill me,
I still weaken before the female
And lose balance in the council chamber.
My heart's desire
Is strength and poise
Under any condition
And in all circumstances –
Under inward stress
Or outer duress.
Learning and a steadfast purpose
Account for much
But nothing succeeds
In the absence of merciful good spirit.
I grow old and agree
With right cradled in good,
Sex harnessed by love,
Youth tended by maturity.

*

5

What we owe our parents,
Since we have taken the big
Step to realization of ourselves,
Defines the value of manners.
The blood tie is encompassed by
The spirit tie, consequently
A unique relation is available;
No need for insult or injury.
The generous act – the seemly word –
At worst they are people with a
    just claim to our honourable attitude,
At best true friends,
Mindful of us as their equals.

When a parent passes on,
Then we understand the
    nature of the connection:
Grief wells up from secret places,
We are shocked where we neglected.
Our children observe us critically,
They take our attitude to heart.
Thus error is transmitted,
From generation to generation –
Or influence of good example.

How we serve their memory:
This makes for enriching history
Or for pitfalls to our progress.

*

6 – 8

Filial piety – be mindful of this –
Springs spontaneously
From painfully acquired good habit.
From the blood connection
Expect only spur and correction.
Hatred of the progenitor proves only
That the son of man must be raised.

*

9

Do not be misled by the quiet demeanour,
By the lack of reaction in the man next to you.
Speak as though you were speaking to god
That perhaps in the silence a soul may prosper.

*

10

Know your companion,
Discover his worth,
So that you may unite with him
In secret companionship.

*

11

The Master said, He who by reanimating
The Old can gain knowledge of
The New is fit to be a teacher.
                              transl. A. Waley

*

12

Would you utilize a human being –
That rare breed with soul and good spirit?
Would you use your fist to pound a nail in?
Or would you approach him in delicate courtship,
Like a dove its mate,
Hoping for unification towards life?

*

13

Day by day I struggle, my god,
Away from hypocrisy – towards integrity.

*

14

Practice circumspection
Lest you mistake an ornament
For the heart of the world.

*

15

The knowledge that is our body,
The learning that is our practical awareness,
These two go hand in hand,
Like the rope passed from left to right.
The head alone is dead,
Bandying cause and sequence;
Tangled in a swoon of self,
The heart alone is evil.
Daily our human nature
Dies in reality
That we may be real.

*

16

Dedication to the merciful spirit
Prohibits competition on the market.
Espouse community
And regret the self.
Not for the man of wisdom, these
Private pursuits, public endeavours.
Adultery undermines the foundation.

*

17

The expert who publicly confesses to an ignorance
May well have progressed to wisdom.
Truth comes to fruition as in dream,
But then eat.
Knowledge is not stored in computers
But as your body when you own it.

*

18

Jesus as the historic
Definition of our natural resources
Obviates the social virtues.
Private and public,
Totally separate finally,
Become one in communal spirit.

The multitude of laws
Is replaced by the one
For him who finds his reward.

*

19 – 21

Always they suppose that
Changing the world
Is a worthwhile ambition.
No,
Personal example effects improvement,
In all walks of life.

The ruling classes,
The common people –
These are outmoded categories.
Instead
Humanity and popularity
Are the contemporary choices.

*

22

When I speak, let me be mindful
Of the connection between my words and myself.
All too often I babble
As if talk were cheap.

What a man says
Comforts those around him
Or dissipates their strength;
Strengthens those around him
Or brings into disrepute.

Certainly we can trust a man
Whose upright mind has been
Trained to an orderly speech.

Equally it is by trusting a man
That we help him become more reliable.

*

23

I can recall the time
When the past came to lie
Restful before my inner eye.
My memory had been extinct.

Today I realize that
Predictions of the future are
Vain sacrifices of the day.

*

from Book III

2

'Feeble trunk, heavy branches' –
Is this not the modern dilemma?
What can our machines tell us
Of the double-sided soul?
Since we ignore the mysteries,
How can our officers be deep,
Except in deception?

As we suspect our falsity
We don the mantle of pretension,
Polishing the outside of the cup
To a high sheen, that
It may reflect the divinity.
In our bones the demons
Celebrate a shallow victory.

Holy vision of society,
The apex of the corporate pyramid
Anchored in the faultless heaven,
Nostalgia for a golden past
Or luxurious goal in the future –
Oh that our present dimension
Should not cause us to lose heart
As we contemplate the realities!

*

3

No such thing as a good man,
This we know now,
After painful experience,
Bitter disappointment of our foolishness,
The hard earned liberty
At last for the freedom of good action.

The variety of overblown words,
Culture, the Arts, Civilization,
Cannot conceal our hunger,
Our secret thirst for the truth,
Essence of all our striving,
Reason for all our diseases.

Choose your celebrities carefully,
The actress, the pop-star, the evangelist,
As they lick their charismatic fingers
After meals of questionable fare.
Look for the genuine human being
In the works you select for enjoyment.

Even belief becomes fashionable
When tradition totters and sinks.
Faith in humanity is extinguished
For the lack of men and women.
Monsters bestride the stage,
Commanding popular attention.

*

4

Let us reflect now on society,
Ancient, modern and contemporary.
There it was ritual of existence.
Then came intrusion of conscience.
Now that we live from within,
Society pertains to the extraneous.
With dignity we are at ease
Among those who think otherwise.

Separation of private from public
Signifies the modern tragedy.
We exist in a kind of light
But insist on a sort of darkness.
The way we openly behave
Does not often reflect how we are.
Frequently we reinvent ourselves
Or manipulate our virtual surroundings.

A contemporary man has no need
To calculate his behaviour or conduct,
Outwardly where convention dictates
Or inwardly where 'self' is known,
For always his manner is spontaneous,
Based freely on works of preparation
And the habit of his spirit is such
That his action is at once a celebration.

*

5

Always the barbarians,
Wherever they crop up,
Bring with them a natural authority.
In our age the barbarians are fifth columnists;
They blow themselves up in public.
Their belief in their god is quite astonishing,
So is their contempt for 'this life'.
'They have kept their princes.'
This means that bureaucracy
Has not replaced the word of honour,
Nor has the love of 'the great man'
Given way to cynical disillusionment.
All the same
Today's barbarians are
Tomorrow's decadents
And the clock will not be turned back.
We are stuck with our position in history
Unless we bail out
And drift down to earth.
Then, when dynasty is usurped
And the rebel crowns himself,
We nod friendly encouragement
And get on with the business of living.

*

6

In the old days it mattered who it was
That made offerings on Mount Prominence.
Today anyone can shinny to the top of Everest
And throw his garbage into the crevasses.
Mt. Athos is not half shrouded in divinity
But material, molecular, like any other thing.

Surely its worthy of being called progress
That god no longer straddles the high places
But what about our fury at being saddled
With bad conscience within inches of
                          one another's faces?
Ask the priests, can they save us from that?
Alas, they are bound to say: "We cannot."

Nothing can kill the desire to worship
But who will point us in the right direction?
Finally, when we see how little children
Lift up their faces with a questioning look,
We refuse to despair, for surely
That same look will eventually rouse our souls.

*

7

This is the burning question:
How to retain the contemporary spirit
fresh in one's vitals.
Inquire into the vice
That most readily causes us to neglect it,
Such as for example victory and triumph
If divorced from the game,
The honourable test of strength,
Not thirst for supremacy.

Ever prone to extinction
We cling to the gift of life.
Evil enters the heart willingly,
Why should we behave carelessly,
Not testing every foothold
But failing to respect the opponent
And suddenly we take darkness for light,
The good messenger for bad news.

*

8

Our application to history,
Our use of tradition
Our interpretation of ancient texts,
Of myths, legends and so-called
Holy writ, who will teach us
The profitable stance,
The expedient handhold,
The perfect vantage point?

Images and symbols
Store up the treasure
For each new age but
One testimony shines brightest,
Concealing beneath literary mediocrity
The secret of human being,
The truth of personal behaviour,
The perfection of speech.

*

9

When studying how to behave
To gain the greatest good,
We look for role models
But finally we must search
In our human heart,
Where the honourable intention
Can displace the cynical expedient.

Shall we condemn the past
For withdrawing its gold?
Shall we disparage the times
For a shortfall from ideals?
When old standards fail
Let the scholar step aside
For the poet and the philosopher.

*

10

Truly it's hard to stand by
When they make their choices:
Of individual over person,
Of marriage over friendship,
Of family over community –
(The preference debases both.)
Of a religion over religion,
Of tradition over history,
Of Society over courtesy –
(The preference debases both.)
Of nation over country,
Of world over earth,
Of system over universe –
(The preference debases both.)

Is it enough to look away?
Yes, sometimes that is quite enough.

*

11

Father of a family, then of a tribe,
Then perhaps of a nation, even of a race –
However in the end we know
The father of the human race
As merely some mythic progenitor,
Conceived by every tribe in its own way,
Not a source of strength,
Merely assurance against the panic
Of being without a beginning.

He who defines himself
Not in terms of a lesser being
Nor in comparison to the dead
May knock on the door of the loving father,
Who precedes and supersedes time
As a source of strength indeed.
Whom do you choose as your ancestor?
Who has been and done for you
That which is worth being and doing?

There are those who follow
And those who wait, also
Those who follow one day and wait the next,
So that all manner may be fulfilled.
But the power of powers is faith,
Is an uncommon trust in being
Which commands all things
And causes their obedience,
Obviating all sacrifice.

*

12

Today we no longer sacrifice
but we worship.
Merciful spirit is always present.
Worship in reality and your only concern is
the absence of self,
the negation of self,
the denial of self.

With your self present
how can you worship merciful spirit of love?

*

13

First a full belly, then heaven,
Say those who have been misled
For they mean: The official God is a waste of
time
And there they have clearly exonerated them-
selves.

Expiation, propitiation – justification:
Let these be viewed in the light of resurrection
When things are made new.
Then the hearth is the altar.

*

14

Let those who write history
Know what service they do
To those who live now.

In a sense we all stride into the past
And owe it to ourselves
Not to make matters worse but better.

*

15

It is nothing but good manners
That we ask questions when we enter another coun-
try.
Neither their customs nor their habits are ours
So by suspending our judgment
We demonstrate a true courtesy of the heart.

*

16

Being right is not the same as doing good.
Beating your opponent is not the same as
persuading him.
Some do more good being weak than
others who are strong.
However let us not confuse
goodness with doing good.

The moderns impress themselves
on an uncertain future.
Contemporary men are impressed by
the certainties of the past.

*

17

Perhaps a time was when
The seasons meant more than a passage of time
Those technologically most advanced
Are least in the know about earth symbols.

Much that was culturally
useful a thousand year ago
is still useful now.

*

18

Are we temped to honour
those who are not honourable?
Scoundrels in high office
tempt us to cynicism.
Also we are tempted to let a
capable public servant get on with it.

Why not treat those who
labour on our behalf with
respect and forbearance.

*

19

The ruler and his ministers
are they not all flesh and blood?
Why must policy differ from value?
In a democracy, let the ruler
live among the people
and not be overly guided by the press.
Let the ministers be of one accord
in the name of 'true expediency'.

*

20

The golden mean in preparation
and then the single faithful will,
that is how we do good nowadays.

*

21

So much comes down to
our attitude to what has passed.
Here we have before us
an immense logic of the will.
Time itself censures and corrects.
In that spirit let us remember.

*

22-26

When we look at those who hold high office
do we not see individuals at he beck and call
of popular mediocrity, of a mediocre populace?
The messianic ruler has come and gone and come
again
and still they behave as if nothing had changed.
Truly we live on holy ground and ignore it.
The master teaches those who acknowledge him.

*

From Book IV

1

No man is good.
Nonetheless there are some who
sincerely strive to do good.
Among them are those who have wisdom
And who set a good example
In their neighbourhood, in their community.
Those who accept them benefit from their wisdom.
A wise man does not so much look for
others who are wise but rather for
Those who might benefit from his wisdom.

*

2

We endure adversity due to
strength of character acquired through
knowledge and understanding of
truth applied in practical reality.

We enjoy prosperity while we
demonstrate a ready willingness to
relinquish it for a good cause.

What is goodness other than good will
which pays, no matter what.

*

3,4

Those we like, those we dislike,
tempt us to injustice.
Once we have begun to love,
such temptation is powerless.
Indeed is there much to choose
between good will and love?

*

5

The way, what we call the way,
is surely dictated by the truth in our heart,
either by birth or acquired.
Best not to profess it but simply to walk it.

Him who desires to walk the way of truth
we call a human being.
The truth is for him a personal companion,
who encourages and teaches,
                    who comforts and heals.

Certainly a human being would cease to be so
if he betrayed that companion.

*

6

Let us not confuse
human beings with machines.
We strive and struggle,
we fail and repair our failures,
we learn, and forget, and learn once more.

An increasing power for doing good
is the goal of our adventure.
Our strength is often increased most successfully
during moments of weakness.

In reality nothing is asked of us
that exceeds our human capacity.

*

7

Once we have identified a fault in ourselves,
we are close to a remedy.
The removal of a fault is
always an additional facility.

Do we look for faults in ourselves?
No, they show up soon enough –
however only while we act
and especially while we act passionately.

*

8

Let him who has ears hear:
The light of day is a blessing.

* * *
* *
*